THE EASY
BOOK OF
SETS

THE EASY BOOK OF SETS

BY DAVID C. WHITNEY
ILLUSTRATED BY TONY FORDE

FRANKLIN WATTS, INC.
NEW YORK ▪ 1972

ALSO BY THE AUTHOR

The Easy Book of Division
The Easy Book of Fractions
The Easy Book of Multiplication
The Easy Book of Numbers and Numerals
Let's Find Out About Addition
Let's Find Out About Subtraction

Library of Congress Cataloging in Publication Data

Whitney, David C
    The easy book of sets.

    (The Easy books series)
    SUMMARY: Explains in text and diagrams the
concept of sets in mathematics.
    1. Set theory–Juvenile literature. [1. Set theory]
I. Forde, Tony, illus. II. Title.
PZ10.W59Eat   511'.3   70-39841
ISBN 0-531-02554-3

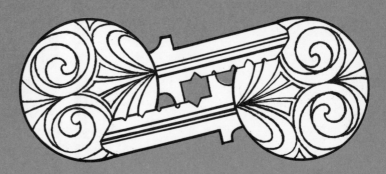

THE EASY
BOOK OF
SETS

A SET is a group of things.
All the animals in a pet shop window are a SET.

7

All the coins in the boy's hand are a SET.

This family is a SET.

When we write the name of a set, we always use a capital
   letter.
This picture is a set of pets. So we can call the set,
                    Set *P*.

10

PET STORE

Because this is a set of coins, we call the set,
Set *C*.

What would you call this set?
Remember to use a capital letter for the name of the set.
Because the set is a family, you would call it
Set *F*.

Each of the things in a set is called a MEMBER.

The cat, the dog, and the parrot are the MEMBERS of this set of pets.

To list, or write, the names of the members of a set, we use lower case (or small) letters. The members of this set of pets are *c* for the cat, *d* for the dog, and *p* for the parrot.

We can say:

    This set of pets has a cat, a dog, and a parrot.

Or we can write:

    Set $P = \{c, d, p\}$.

When we write the names of all the members of a set, we
    enclose the members in *braces* $\{\ \}$.

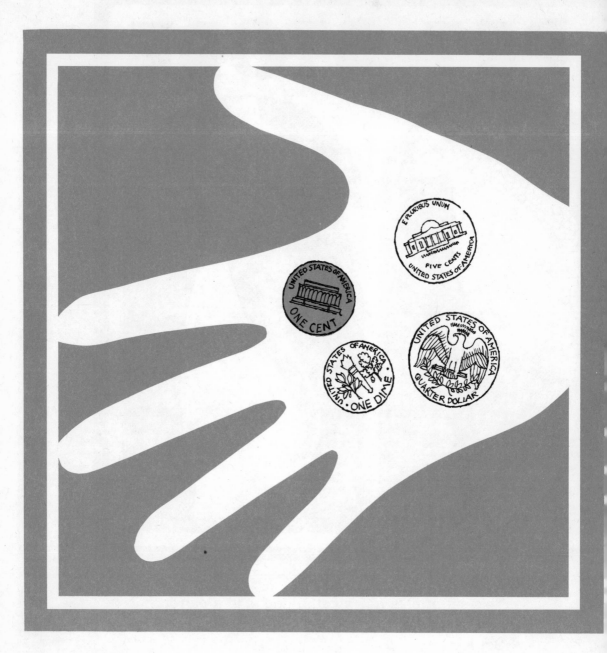

The members of this set of coins are a cent, a nickel, a dime, and a quarter. We use lower case letters for the names of the members of the set: *c* (cent), *n* (nickel), *d* (dime), *q* (quarter). And we put braces around them to show that they are members of a set.

Set $C = \{c, n, d, q\}$.

On a separate sheet of paper, write the name of this set and the names of the members of the set. Then compare your answer to the one below.

Correct answer:

Set $F = \{f, m, b, g\}$.

Because the set is a family, we call it Set F, with a capital letter. We use lower case letters to show the members of the family: f (father), m (mother), b (boy), and g (girl).

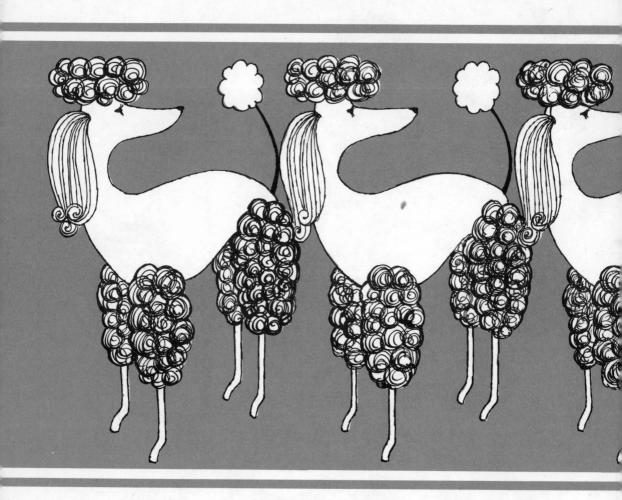

This is a set of dogs. It has five dogs as members of the
set.

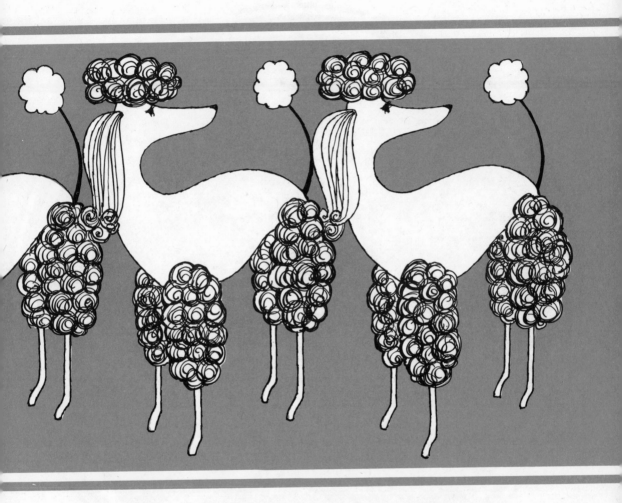

Any set that has an exact number of members is called a
FINITE set.

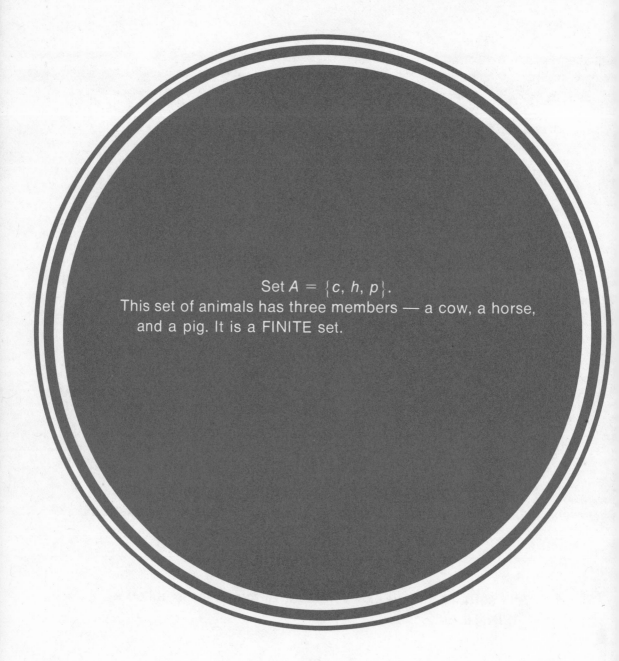

Set $A = \{c, h, p\}$.
This set of animals has three members — a cow, a horse, and a pig. It is a FINITE set.

22

23

This is a set of stars in the sky. It has so many members that we cannot count them all.

Any set that has an endless number of members is called an INFINITE set. After listing a few of the members, you write three dots. The three dots show that you could continue writing additional members to the set.

Set $S = \{a, b, c, \ldots\}$.

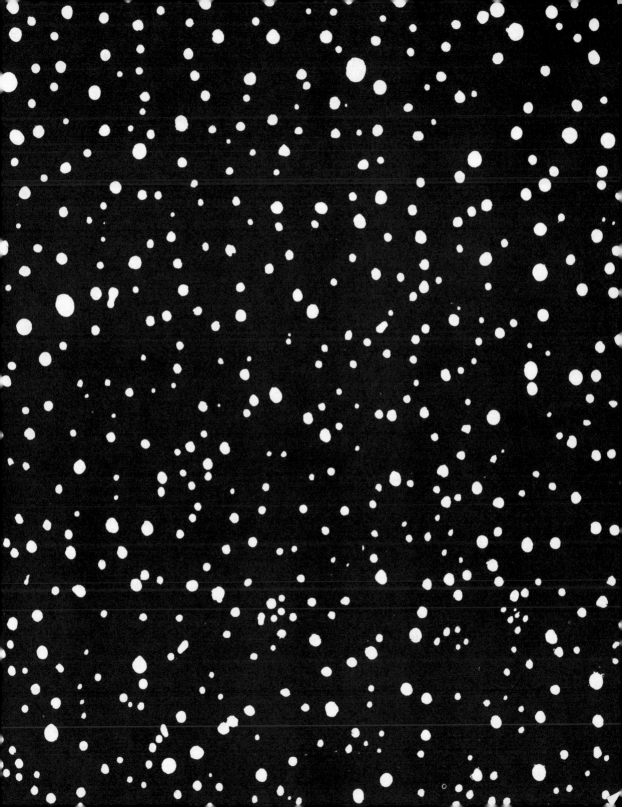

Sometimes sets have no members. A set without any members is called an EMPTY set, or a NULL set.

The set of all the animals in this pet shop window is an EMPTY set because there are no animals in the window.

When you write the names of the members of an empty set, you leave an empty space between the braces. This shows that there are no members. Or you can write the names of the members of an empty set by showing the symbol $\emptyset$, a zero with a slanted line through it.

$$\text{Set } A = \{\ \}.$$

or

$$\text{Set } A = \emptyset.$$

The set of all the people in this swimming pool is an empty
set, or a null set, because there are no people in the
swimming pool.

$$\text{Set } P = \{\ \} = \emptyset.$$

On a separate sheet of paper, write the answers to these problems. Then compare your answers to the correct answers on this page.

1. Write out the set and its members for this family.
2. Write out the set and its members for all the circles.
3. Write out the set and its members for all the people who are looking out of this window.
4. The set in Problem 1 is (a) finite, (b) infinite, or (c) empty.
5. The set in Problem 2 is (a) finite, (b) infinite, or (c) empty.
6. The set in Problem 3 is (a) finite, (b) infinite, or (c) empty.

These are the correct answers to the problems.

1. Set $F = \{f, m, b\}$.
2. Set $C = \{a, b, c, \ldots\}$.
3. Set $P = \{\ \} = \emptyset$.
4. The set of family members is FINITE, because there are an exact number of members.
5. The set of all the circles is INFINITE, because there is an endless number.
6. The set of all the people looking out of the window is an EMPTY set, because there are no people looking out of the window.

30

Here are three cats in one set and three dogs in another
  set. Because each set has the *same number*, the sets
  are EQUIVALENT.

You could say: The set of cats is *equivalent* to the set of
  dogs, because there is the same number of cats and
  of dogs.

The symbol $\longleftrightarrow$ means *equivalent*, having the same number.

So you would write:

$$C \longleftrightarrow D.$$

The set of four flowers is EQUIVALENT to the set of four rabbits, because each set has the same number of members.

$$F \longleftrightarrow R.$$

The set of five giraffes eating leaves from the tree in a park is the *same* as the set of giraffes riding in the boat. Because each set has the *identical members*, the two sets are EQUAL.

If Set *A* is the five giraffes eating leaves and if Set *B* is the five giraffes riding in a boat, then we can say that Set *A* EQUALS Set *B*. Or we can write:

$$A = B.$$

Set *C* is a group of three boys walking on a fence.

Set *D* is the *same* group of three boys throwing rocks into a pond.

Because each set has the *same members*, the sets are EQUAL.

$$C = D.$$

1. Is Set *O*, the set of owls, equal to or equivalent to Set *C*, the set of clocks?
2. Is Set *A*, the set of girls on the seesaw, equal to Set *B*, the set of girls riding bicycles?

3. Is Set *C*, the set of dogs chasing the cat, equal to Set *D*, the set of dogs eating?
4. Is Set *B*, the set of books, equal to or equivalent to Set *P*, the set of pencils?

These are the answers to the problems.

1. *O* $\longleftrightarrow$ *C*. (The set of owls is EQUIVALENT to the set of clocks, because each set has the *same number*.)

2. *A* = *B*. (The set of girls on the seesaw is EQUAL to the set of girls riding bicycles, because the *same girls* are the members of each set.)

3. *C* = *D*. (The set of dogs chasing the cat is EQUAL to the set of dogs eating, because the *same dogs* are the members of each set.)

4. *B* $\longleftrightarrow$ *P*. (The set of books is EQUIVALENT to the set of pencils, because each set has the *same number*.)

When two sets are joined together to make one set, it is
  called the UNION of the sets.
When the set of two flowers is joined to the set of five
  flowers, it makes a set of seven flowers.
You can say: *A union B* makes a set of seven flowers.
You write *A union B* as $A \cup B$.
So,

$$A = \{a, b\}.$$
$$B = \{c, d, e, f, g\}.$$
$$A \cup B = \{a, b, c, d, e, f, g\}.$$

42

Set *C* is four kangaroos. Set *D* is four kangaroos. *C union D* is eight kangaroos.

$$C = \{h, i, j, k\}.$$
$$D = \{l, m, n, o\}.$$
$$C \cup D = \{h, i, j, k, l, m, n, o\}.$$

Set *E* is a horse, a cow, a goat, and a pig in a farmyard.
Set *F* is the goat, the pig, a rooster, and a duck in a truck
  on the way to market. The same goat and the same pig
  are in Set *E* and Set *F*.
These sets are called OVERLAPPING sets. Each set has
  some of the members of the other set — the goat and
  the pig are in each of these sets.

In the union of overlapping sets, the joined set always has
a smaller number of members than in the two sets
counted separately. That is because the members that
are in both sets are not counted twice.

Therefore, in *E union F* there are only six animals — a
horse, a cow, a goat, a pig, a rooster, and a duck.

$$E = \{h, c, g, p\}.$$
$$F = \{g, p, r, d\}.$$
$$E \cup F = \{h, c, g, p, r, d\}.$$

The five books on the shelf are Set *G*.
The two books carried away by the girl are Set *H*.

Because *G* and *H* are OVERLAPPING SETS, *G union H* has only five members — the five books that originally were on the shelf.

$$G = \{a, b, c, d, e\}.$$
$$H = \{a, b\}.$$
$$G \cup H = \{a, b, c, d, e\}.$$

Set *E* is a horse, a cow, a goat, and a pig in a farmyard.
Set *F* is the goat, the pig, a rooster, and a duck in a truck
on the way to market. The same goat and the same pig
are in Set *E* and Set *F*.

The INTERSECTION of the sets tells which members are
in both sets. So the INTERSECTION of *E* and *F* is the
goat and the pig — the two members that are in both
sets.

You can say: *E intersection F* is the goat and the pig.

You can write this as: $E \cap F = \{g, p\}$.

$$E = \{h, c, g, p\}.$$
$$F = \{g, p, r, d\}.$$
$$E \cap F = \{g, p\}.$$

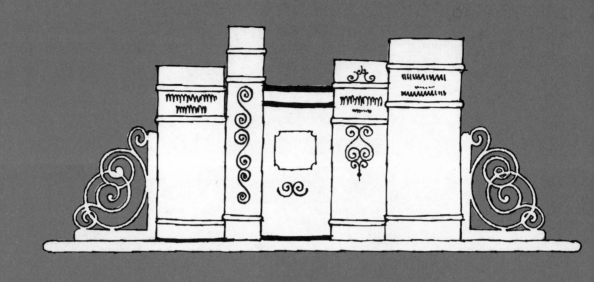

The five books on the shelf are Set *G*.
The two books carried away by the girl are Set *H*.

Two of the books are in both sets. So, *G intersection H*, or
G ∩ *H*, is the two books, or {*a*, *b*}.

$$G = \{a, b, c, d, e\}.$$
$$H = \{a, b\}.$$
$$G \cap H = \{a, b\}.$$

REMEMBER THAT ∪ MEANS *UNION* AND ∩ MEANS
INTERSECTION.

The three houses are Set *A*.
The four cars are Set *B*.
A union B, or $A \cup B$, has the same total number of houses
and cars as in both sets counted separately. This is because there are no members that are in both sets.

A intersection B, or *A* ∩ *B*, is an empty set. There are no members that are in both sets.

$$A = \{a, b, c\}.$$
$$B = \{d, e, f, g\}.$$
$$A \cup B = \{a, b, c, d, e, f, g\}.$$
$$A \cap B = \{\ \} = \emptyset.$$

The two flowers are Set C.
The four birds are Set D.
C union D, or C ∪ D, includes all the flowers and all the birds, because there are no members that are in both sets.

C intersection D, or $C \cap D$, is an empty set. There are no
members that are in both sets.

$$C = \{h, i\}.$$
$$D = \{j, k, l, m\}.$$
$$C \cup D = \{h, i, j, k, l, m\}.$$
$$C \cap D = \{\ \} = \emptyset.$$

The eight zebras are Set Z.

Three of the zebras are also Set A.

The five remaining members of Set Z are called the COM-
  PLEMENT of Set A. The symbol A' is read as A prime
  and means "the *complement* of Set A."

So we know that A′, or the *complement* of Set A, has as members the five zebras from Set Z that are not members of Set A.

$$Z = \{a, b, c, d, e, f, g, h\}.$$
$$A = \{f, g, h\}.$$
$$A' = \{a, b, c, d, e\}.$$

The three monkeys of Set N are part of the seven monkeys of Set M. The *complement* of Set N, or N', has as members the remaining four monkeys.

$$M = \{l, m, n, o, p, q, r\}.$$
$$N = \{p, q, r\}.$$
$$N' = \{l, m, n, o\}.$$

When a smaller set is part of a larger set, the COMPLEMENT of the smaller set is made up of all the remaining members of the larger set that are not already included in the smaller set.

On a separate sheet of paper, write the answers to these problems. Then compare your answers to the correct answers on this page.

Set A is four puppies — a, b, c, d.

Set B is five puppies — e, f, g, h, i.

1. $A \cup B = ?$
2. $A \cap B = ?$
3. Set A is (a) a finite set, or (b) an infinite set?
4. $C \cup D$ means (a) C union D, or (b) C intersection D?
5. $C \cap D$ means (a) C union D, or (b) C intersection D?
6. $E \longleftrightarrow F$ means (a) Set E is equivalent to Set F, or (b) Set E is equal to Set F?
7. $E = F$ means (a) Set E is equal to Set F, or (b) Set E is equivalent to Set F?

These are the answers to the problems.

1. $A \cup B = \{a, b, c, d, e, f, g, h, i\}$.
2. $A \cap B = \{ \} = \emptyset$.
3. Set A is a finite set.
4. $C \cup D$ means C union D.
5. $C \cap D$ means C intersection D.
6. $E \longleftrightarrow F$ means Set E is equivalent to Set F.
7. $E = F$ means Set E is equal to Set F.

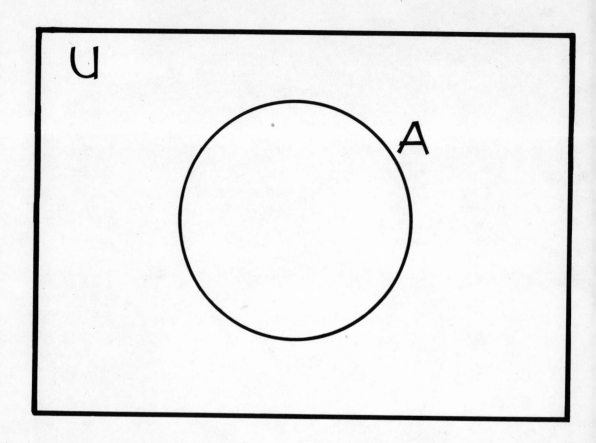

Mathematicians use diagrams called *Venn* diagrams to represent sets.

The large rectangle stands for all the members of a set being used in a particular problem. The name of this large set is *U*. The *U* is placed in the upper left-hand corner of the diagram.

The circle in the middle of the diagram stands for a smaller set that includes some of the members of Set *U*. The smaller set is named *A* by the letter to the upper right of the circle.

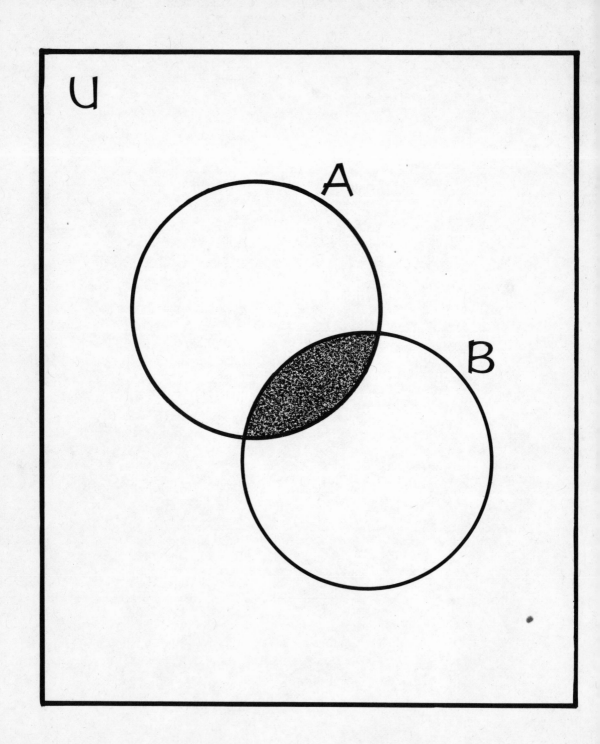

This Venn diagram shows two overlapping sets, *A* and *B*. The shaded part where the circles overlap shows *A intersection B*, or *A* ∩ *B*.

The diagram would help solve a problem such as this: There are twenty families that live on one block. Six of the families buy groceries at Mr. Schmidt's store. Eight families buy clothes at Mr. Carol's store. Nine families do not buy at either store. How many families on the block buy at both stores?

U = families that live on the block.

A = families that buy from Mr. Schmidt.

B = families that buy from Mr. Carol.

A ∩ *B* = the number of families who buy at both stores.

Answer:

U = 20.

A = 6.

B = 8.

A + *B* = 14 families. But 9 families don't buy at either store. 20 − 9 = 11. So only 11 families do any buying at all at these stores. 14 − 11 = 3. So there must be an overlap of 3 families.

A ∩ *B* = 3.

On a separate sheet of paper, write the answers to these problems. Then compare your answers to the correct answers on the next page.

1. Is Set P, the set of pears, equal to ($=$) or equivalent to ($\longleftrightarrow$) Set L, the set of ladybugs?

2. Is Set A, the set of kittens playing with the yarn, equal to Set B, the set of kittens sleeping in the basket?

$A = \{c, t, s\}$ (chair, table, sofa).
$B = \{c, b, g\}$ (chair, boy, girl).

3. $A \cup B = ?$
4. $A \cap B = ?$

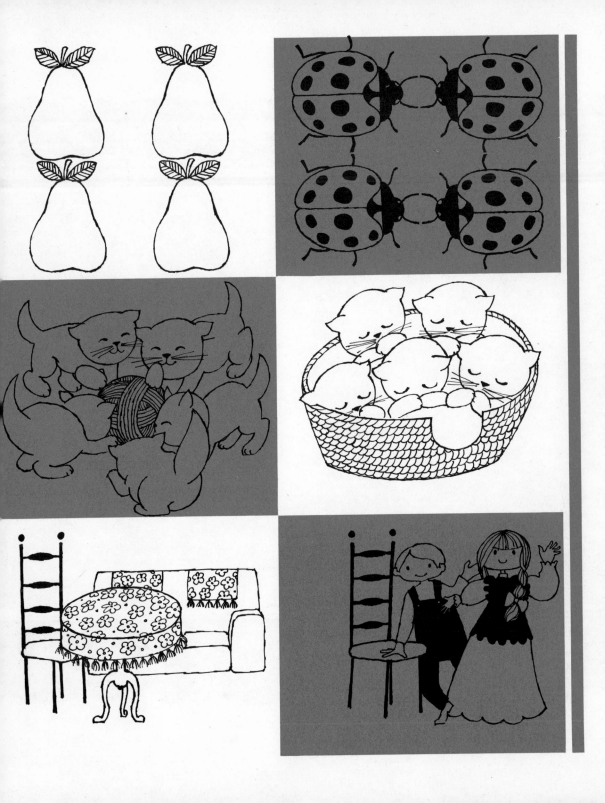

These are the answers to the problems on the previous page.

1. $P \longleftrightarrow L$.　　(Set *P* is the equivalent of Set *L* because each set has the *same number* of members.)

2. $A = B$.　　(Set *A* equals Set *B* because each set has the same five kittens as members.)

3. $A \cup B = \{c, t, s, b, g\}$.

4. $A \cap B = \{c\}$. (The chair is the only member that is in both Set *A* and Set *B*.)

THINGS TO REMEMBER

- A SET is a group of things.
- When we write the name of a set, we always use a capital letter.
- Each of the things in a set is called a MEMBER.
- When we write the names of the members of a set, we always use lower case (or small) letters.
- When we write the names of the members of a set, we always enclose the members with braces { }.
- Any set that has an exact number of members is called a FINITE set.
- Any set that has an endless number of members is called an INFINITE set. To show that a set is infinite, you list several of the members and then write three dots — {a, b, c, . . .}.
- A set without any members is called an EMPTY set or a NULL set. To show that a set is empty, you can leave an empty space between the braces or you can use a zero with a slanted line through it — { } = $\emptyset$.

70

MORE THINGS TO REMEMBER

- When each set has the same number of members, the sets are EQUIVALENT. $A \longleftrightarrow B$ says Set A is *equivalent* to Set B.
- When two sets have the same members, the sets are EQUAL. $A = B$ says Set A is *equal* to Set B.
- When two sets are joined together to make one set, it is called the UNION of the sets. $A \cup B$ says A *union B*.
- When two sets have some of the same members, the sets are called OVERLAPPING sets.
- The INTERSECTION of two sets tells which members are in both sets. $A \cap B$ says A *intersection B*.

ABOUT THE AUTHOR

In simple, easy-to-understand terms, David Whitney introduces the young reader to the fascinating world of mathematics. His other books in this series include *The Easy Book of Multiplication*, *The Easy Book of Division*, *Let's Find Out About Addition*, *The Easy Book of Fractions*, and *The Easy Book of Subtraction*. The author lives in Chappaqua, New York.